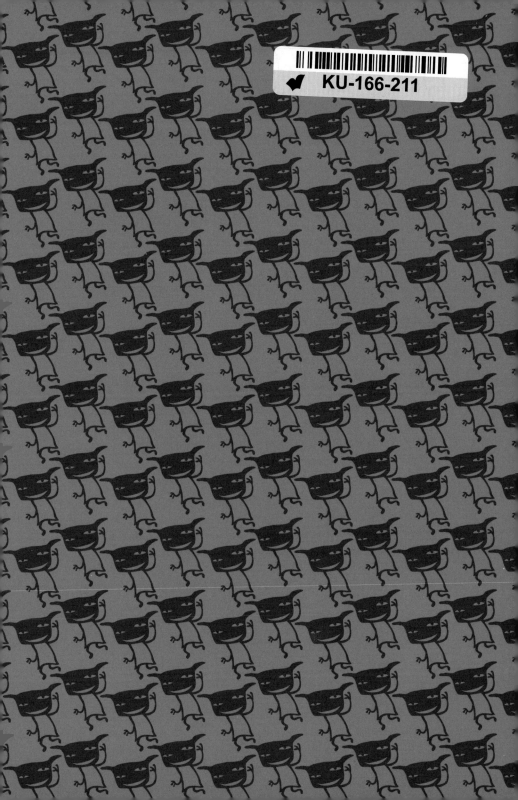

The Bad Book

ARANZI ARONZO

CONTENTS

INTRODUCTION

Hello, I am the Bad Guy.
Because I am the Bad Guy, I do bad things.
I think bad things.
Sometimes I even do some soul-searching.
Bad things are fun.
Bad things are sad.
But,
I am the Bad Guy, so I keep on keeping on.

Hello, I am the Liar.
Because I am the Liar, I lie.
Wait, no!
I do not lie.
I always tell the truth.
I'm no friend of the Bad Guy, no way.
Every day sucks.
I kind of think this book sucks too.

Bad Guy and Crow

Petty Thief

Bad Guy in Winter

Bad Guy in Summer

Bad Guy vs. Liar

1. The Ambush

Bad Guy Loses

Curse of the Bad Guy

Warning:
Do not read if you're sensitive

Bad Guy Shenanigans

If you trip on
a rock

That rock is
the Bad Guy

If your stomach
hurts because
you drank
sour milk

That milk is
the Bad Guy

If it starts
pouring and
you don't
have an
umbrella

That rain is
the Bad Guy

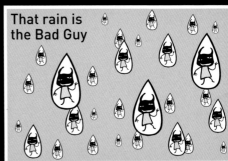

A dream — a bad Bad Guy upgrade

A dream — laundered and hung to dry

A dream — my childhood self looks at me
with a disappointed face

A dream that's just sad

"Stupid idiot!" "Liar♥Meanie"

Bad Guy vs. Liar

2. The Sunset

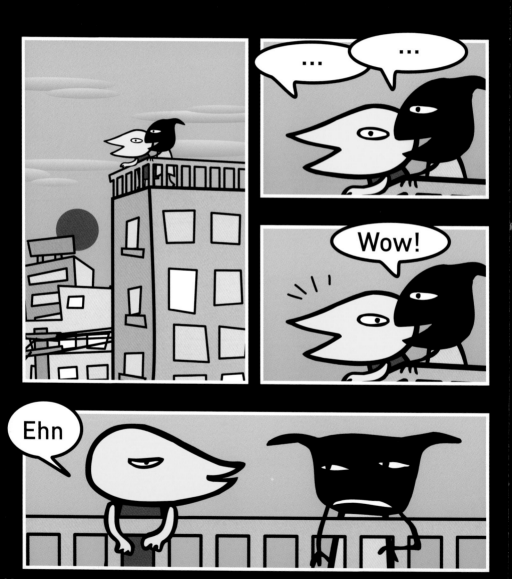

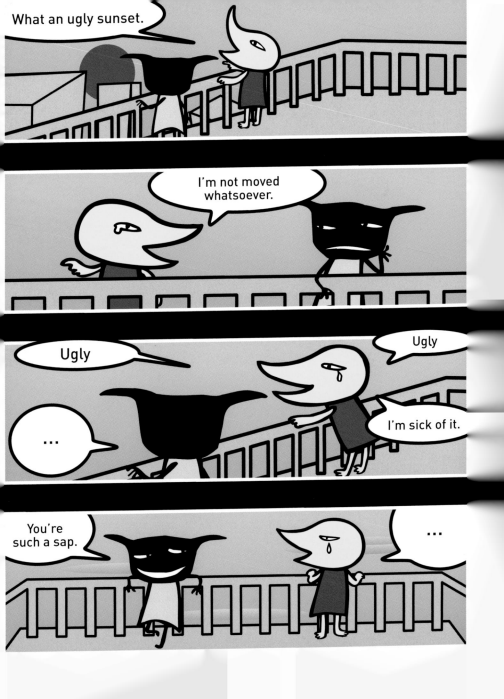

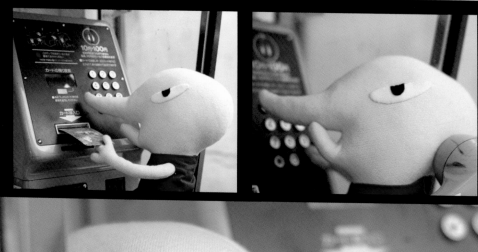

Fancy Bad Guy

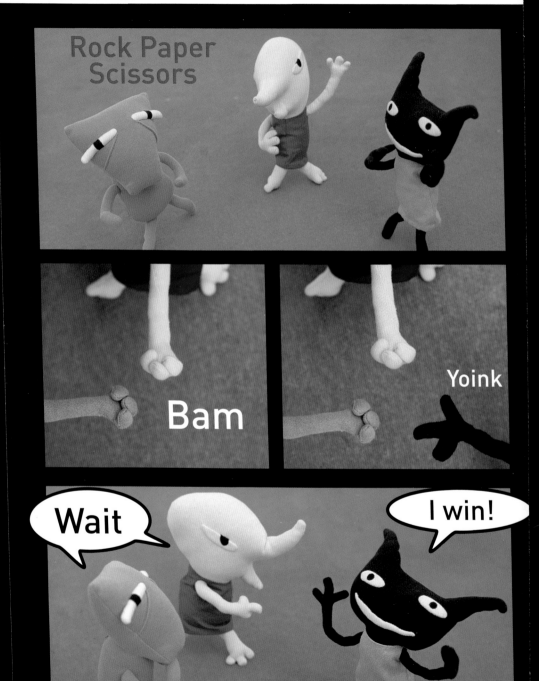

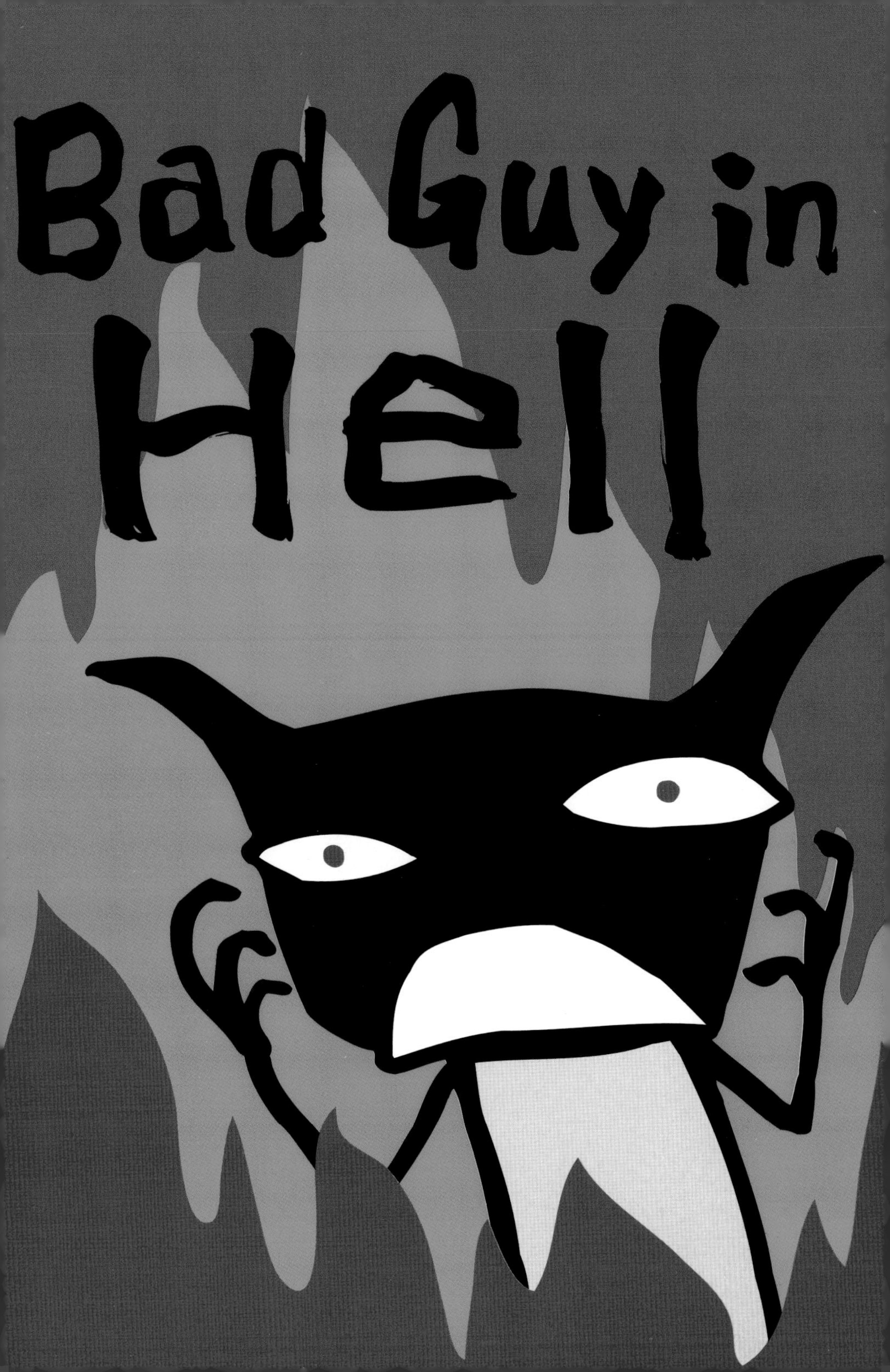
Bad Guy in
Hell

The Lake of Blood pool

Noodles cooked in cauldron of Hell

Bad Guy Fashion

Bad Guy Diet

and then

Everything in moderation!

The Bad GUYS

Bad Guy

Useless

Liar

Inna Rush

Complainer

Dirtie

Sneaky

Cringer

Unlucky

Ann Oying

Sloven

Meanie

Cheapskate

Sarcastic

Gloomy

Tacky

Dirtie

Gloomy and Cringer

Ann Oying

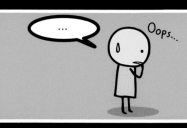

 # Cheapskate

Words I love:
- **Get**
- **Receive**
- **Free**

...You've gotta be brave.

VERY NICE!

Words I loathe:
- **Give**
- **Lend**
- **Treat**

A strong will is needed to avoid all that.

OH! NO!

Complainer

Ugh, it's morning. Dangit, do I have to get up?

Every freakin' morning I have to brush my teeth. It's such a hassle. Freakin' cavities.

What the?! What do those politicians think they're doing? And those junior high brats nowadays!

Grumble grumble Tsk grumble So annoying grumble grumble What's the deal? Grumble grumble grumble Uh-oh I told you I didn't want to! Grumble grumble

Oh man, I'm so exhausted. Walking really takes it out of me.

My legs are so tired. I'm getting old. I hate it.

Grumble grumble dangit! Grumble grumble Oh well grumble grumble What did you say? Grumble grumble That jerk! Grumble grumble Not again! Grumble grumble grumble sigh...

You call this food? It tastes so awful! Isn't there something even better than this? remotely

There is nothing good on TV. It's all so boring and idiotic, so who's letting it run on like this, geez. Who's watching this crap anyway?

Ugh, it's already nighttime. Gotta go to sleep dangit. Grumble grumble.

Zzzzz

Sneaky

How sneaky!

Eh heh heh!

You are so sneaky!

I don't know about that.

You are sneaky.

Ha ha ha

You are a Sneaky.

Oh yeah?

About the Characters

Bad Guy
Always doing bad
Also kind of timid
and easily flattered

Liar
Always telling lies
Also thoughtful
of his friends and
altogether ok

Meanie
Always being mean
Also upset that
he didn't get much
face time or chances
to be mean

PROFILE

ARANZI ARONZO

Aranzi Aronzo is a company that "makes what it feels like the way it feels like and then sells the stuff." Established in 1991 in Osaka. Kinuyo Saito and Yoko Yomura team. Other than original miscellany, Aranzi Aronzo also makes picture books and exhibits. Other books include *Aranzi Aronzo Ltd., The Aranzi Hour, Aranzi Machine Gun,* and *The Tamahiyo Picture Book Series.*

http://www.aranziaronzo.com

Translation — Anne Ishii

Copyright © 2007 by Aranzi Aronzo

All rights reserved.

Published by Vertical, Inc., New York.

Originally published in Japanese as *Warui Hon* by Kadokawa Shoten, Tokyo, 2002.

ISBN 1-932234-69-1/978-1-932234-69-5

Manufactured in Singapore

First American Edition

Vertical, Inc.
www.vertical-inc.com

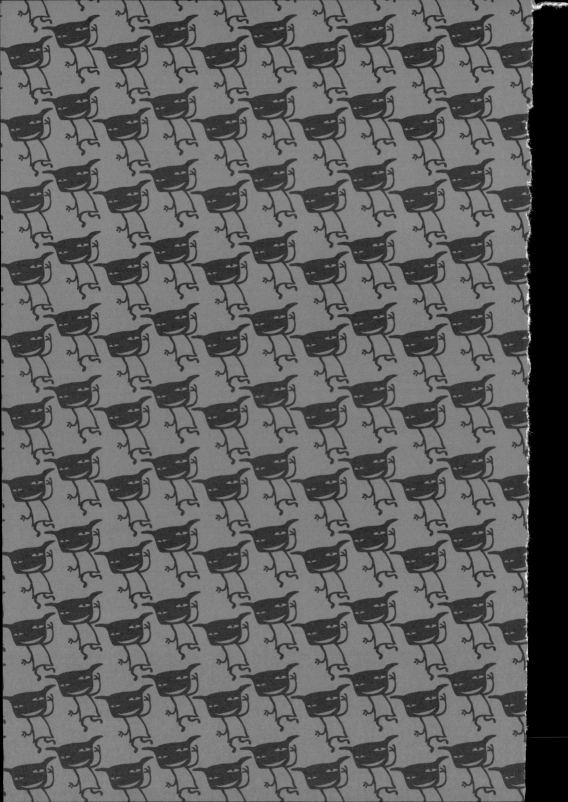